With and love, Denise ♡

The Temple Within llc, 12841 Hillcrest NE, Lowell MI 49331

www.DeniseIwaniw.com

First Edition 2017©

ISBN: 978-0-9886851-6-1

Graphics: Artist, David Fix   www.HearthProductions.com

Editor: Sharon Rosenblum

Photo Credit: Nicole Werner   www.NicoleWernerPhotography.com

Table of Contents

Preface

Dedication

A Word from the Artist

Angels All Around Us

Preface

"Angel": From the Greek word "Angelos," a translation of the Hebrew word "Malakh," originally meaning "Messenger."

Angel of God, my guardian Dear

Angel of God, my guardian dear,

To whom God's love commits me here,

Ever this day be at my side,

To light and guard, to rule and guide.

Amen.

What are angels? The idea of guardian spirits dates back to early civilization and can be found in the belief systems of cultures all around the world. The ancient Assyrians, Greeks, Japanese, Indians and Egyptians are just a few examples of civilizations that had names of individual spirits who watched over and guided every human being.

The existence of angels is an essential element to the four monotheistic religions of the western world: Christianity, Islam, Judaism, and Zoroastrianism. The sacred texts belonging to these faiths teach their followers that angels are as real as the God they serve.

Dedication

This book is dedicated to each and every one of the magnificent children who inhabit Grandmother Earth. May they all come to understand that like the brilliant angels who accompany and guide them, their origins are also to be found in the living Light of God. And may they come to know that they are in fact, related to every living thing that is both seen and unseen throughout the vast expanse of the cosmos and within, the unified field of the Creator's love.

-Denise Iwaniw-Francisco, author

A Word from the Artist

I am grateful to Denise Iwaniw-Francisco for asking me to be a part of the creation of this book. In a class years ago, as Denise was guiding us through a meditation, I saw an angel. It appeared as a purple orb with waves of light eminating from its center. This was one of many early awakenings that Denise has given me. "Angels All Around Us" is the most recent. I hope children of all ages find as much joy in this book as I have.

-David Fix, artist

"Are angels all the same age?" asked seven-year-old Sofia.

"Why do you ask?" responded her elder, wise friend, Dana.

"Because," Sofia went on to explain, "sometimes when I see angels they look like large circles of brightly colored light. Some are purple or blue, others are pink or green and sometimes a little bit of each."

With a great big smile on her face, Dana looked into Sofia's sparkly blue eyes and said, "They sound so beautiful, Sofia!"

"Oh, they are! They also feel very nice when I see them. But that's not the only kind of angel I see, Dana," said Sofia in a joyful voice.

Leaning forward in her seat on her comfy chair in Dana's library, Sofia went on to say, "Some of the angels that I see are very, very large with great big beautiful wings. Others are quite small, with tiny little, colorful wings. These kinds of angels also have twinkly eyes that make me feel happy inside when I see them."

3

4

"Do you feel that these angels are different in age?" Dana asked.

"Yes," said Sofia. "The round shaped angels feel very old to me and the angels with wings feel younger to me. I can't really explain it in words. It's something that I just feel."

6

"Well," Dana offered, "we should always trust our feelings and our intuition, Sofia. Our feelings and our intuition are a gift from the Creator. Our feelings naturally help us to understand what is going around us and inside of us. Intuition is a special sense that helps us to know about something we may not be able to see, but something we can just feel. Does that make sense?"

"It does make sense," replied Sofia. "Sometimes I can feel things and just know about things that other people can't feel or see - like the angels."

"Sofia," Dana replied, " I happen to believe that everything in the universe was made out of pure light and love by the Creator, including angels. I also believe that just like us humans; that animals, plants, minerals and rocks, were also created at the perfect time and at all different times. Just like you and me."

Slapping her dainty right hand to her petite right knee and with a great big smile on her face, Sofia looked at Dana and exclaimed, "Me too!"

10

"Would you like to learn about the Four Mighty Archangels, Sofia?" asked Dana.

Without a moment's hesitation, Sofia responded with a hearty, "Yes!"

Then, snuggling into her comfy chair in Dana's library of art and ancient books, Sofia listened intently as Dana taught her about the Archangels Michael, Uriel, Gabriel and Raphael.

11

Dana leaned back in her beautiful, white wicker arm chair and said, "Let's begin with the Archangel Michael. Some people call him Saint Michael.

Sofia asked, "Why do some people call him Saint Michael?"

"That's a great question, Sofia! The word saint in Latin is sancta, which means 'holy'. People of many faiths believe that these four archangels are holy and therefore are considered to be saints."

Michael's name means, "Who is like God or He who shines like God." He is often referred to as the protector of children, police offers and soldiers. Michael is the defender of Light and goodness.

Whenever we are feeling scared or uncertain, we can call upon St. Michael to come to us and help us feel safe and protected."

13

14

The Archangel Uriel or Saint Uriel's name means, "Light of God." Uriel brings divine light into our lives and helps us to fulfill our dreams and our goals. He helps to heal broken hearts and teaches us about how to forgive ourselves and others.

"It's good to be forgiving, isn't it Dana?"

"It sure is Sofia. Sometimes it's just as important to forgive ourselves as it is to forgive others. Uriel teaches us how to have a gentle heart. The Creator loves us just the way we are, Sofia. Sometimes, we need to remember to love ourselves just the way we are, too."

15

16

The Archangel Gabriel is also known to some as the Archangel St. Gabriel. Gabriel's name means, "Hero of God or God is my strength." Gabriel is the angel known for telling Mary about the coming birth of her son, Jesus and who later said to the shepherds in Bethlehem, "Behold, I bring you good tidings of great joy!" when Jesus was born. St. Gabriel is also the divine messenger who delivered the words of the Koran to the prophet Mohammed.

Sofia smiled broadly and said, "I remember the angel Gabriel from my Christmas play at Sunday School, Dana. My friend Addison got to dress like an angel and play the part of St. Gabriel. She looked so beautiful! I was a shepherd watching sheep in the play. We had so much fun!"

18

The Archangel Saint Raphael's name means, "God heals." He is the angel of healing. Raphael watches over the healing of Grandmother Earth and every living thing that lives upon her. Archangel Raphael helps doctors, nurses, veterinarians and healers of all kinds to be the best healers they can be. We can call upon Raphael when we or someone we know needs healing of their body, mind or spirit. He also helps travelers to have safe journeys.

"Does that mean if I hurt myself on the playground or if I see someone else get hurt that I can ask Raphael for help?"

"That's exactly what it means." Dana replied.

"When we see a sick or injured animal, she continued, we can ask Raphael to help that animal. Raphael is really good at making sure the right person comes along to assist every living thing that is in need of help."

20

"Would you like to learn a very easy and fun exercise to invite the Four Mighty Archangels to be with you each day, Sofia?"

"Yes, please!" was her enthusiastic reply.

"Wonderful! You will need to use your imagination in this exercise. Let me know when you are ready."

"Ready," she proclaimed!

"Okay Sofia," said Dana, "go ahead and close your eyes and repeat after me either out loud or in your heart:

Archangel Saint Michael, thank you for standing at my right-hand side.

Archangel Saint Uriel, thank you for standing in front of me.

Archangel Saint Gabriel thank you for standing at my left-hand side.

Archangel Saint Raphael, thank you for standing behind me.

Thank you all for being with me today."

21

After Sofia finished, Dana then said, "Okay Sofia, now I would like for you to use your imagination and imagine that all four of the Archangels are standing with you, just as you asked them to."

"Dana, I am imagining that the four angels are beautiful, bright lights; blue, purple, pink and green. Archangel Michael is standing on one side and Archangel Gabriel on the other and Archangel Uriel is standing in front of me and Archangel Raphael is behind me."

24

"How do you feel, Sofia?" asked Dana.

Her eyes now gently closed and with a smile on her lips, Sofia said, "I feel really good. The angels feel like friends that are right here with me."

"That's a great way to describe them," said Dana. "They are like friends. Friends who we may not see with our eyes, but friends that we can feel with our heart, Sofia."

Sofia's sparkly blue eyes slowly opened, and she said, "Thank you, Dana, for teaching me about the angels of Light today. May I come back some time and talk to you about faeries and things like that, Dana?"

"You most certainly can, Sofia. For now, remember that you are always loved by the Creator and that the Four Mighty Archangels are only a quiet call away."

And with that, Sofia and Dana stood up to give one another a grateful hug, knowing that the Archangels Michael, Uriel, Gabriel and Raphael were gently hugging them, too.

Sofia could hardly wait to come back to the beautiful library of art and ancient books to learn more about the faeries from her friend, Dana.

Denise Iwaniw

 A native of Georgia, Denise and her family now live in Michigan. A seer of international renown, she facilitates private reading sessions for men, women and children from around the world. Denise facilitates classes and workshops both internationally and in the U.S., in a wide variety of areas, including Reiki, paths to spiritual enlightenment and psychic development. Denise is the co-creator of The Mystic's Heart, co-founder of Star Nations Magazine, Book Publishing and the Star Nations Radio Network. She is also president and founder of Gathering Thunder Foundation. Denise is the founder of The Temple Within llc, Temple Within Publishing and the Temple Within School of Sacred Studies.

You can visit Denise on her website at: www.DeniseIwaniw.com

Archangel pendants available at www.TheMysticsHeart.com

Also from Denise Iwaniw and The Temple Within Publishing:

"Meditations from The Temple Within - Book and Meditation CD"

"Embracing the Mystic Within"

"A Year of Mystic Angels"

"The Mystic Angels Empowerment Deck"

"The Mysteries of Ancient Egypt Empowerment Deck"

"The Totem Animals Empowerment Deck"

"Spirit of Mythology Empowerment Deck"

"Beyond the Veil Lies a Mystic Journey" – Guided Meditation CD

"The Journey of Light – Walking the Reiki Path Reiki Practitioners Guidebook"

"The Reiki Path" - Guided Meditation CD

"Journey to the Temple Within" - Guided Meditation CD

"The Athlete Within" - Guided Meditation CD

Empowerment decks available at www.TheMysticsHeart.com

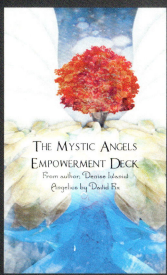
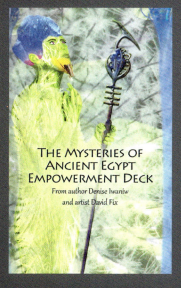